Poetry for Students, Volume 4

Staff

Series Editor: Mary Ruby.

Contributing Editors: Margaret Haerens and Lynn Koch.

Managing Editor: Drew Kalasky.

Research: Victoria B. Cariappa, *Research Team Manager.* Andy Malonis, *Research Specialist.* Julia C. Daniel, Tamara C. Nott, Tracie A. Richardson, and Cheryl L. Warnock, *Research Associates.* Jeffrey Daniels, *Research Assistant.*

Permissions: Susan M. Trosky, *Permissions Manager.* Kimberly F. Smilay, *Permissions Specialist.* Kelly Quin, *Permissions Assistant.*

Production: Mary Beth Trimper, *Production Director.* Evi Seoud, *Assistant Production Manager.* Shanna Heilveil, *Production Assistant.*

Graphic Services: Randy Bassett, *Image Database*

Supervisor. Robert Duncan and Michael Logusz, *Imaging Specialists.* Pamela A. Reed, *Photography Coordinator.* Gary Leach, *Macintosh Artist.*

Product Design: Cynthia Baldwin, *Product Design Manager.* Cover Design: Michelle DiMercurio, *Art Director.* Page Design: Pamela A. E. Galbreath, *Senior Art Director.*

Copyright Notice

Since this page cannot legibly accommodate all copyright notices, the acknowledgments constitute an extension of the copyright notice.

While every effort has been made to secure permission to reprint material and to ensure the reliability of the information presented in this publication, Gale Research neither guarantees the accuracy of the data contained herein nor assumes any responsibility for errors, omissions, or discrepancies. Gale accepts no payment for listing; and inclusion in the publication of any organization, agency, institution, publication, service, or individual does not imply endorsement of the editors or publisher. Errors brought to the attention of the publisher and verified to the satisfaction of the publisher will be corrected in future editions.

This publication is a creative work fully protected by all applicable copyright laws, as well as by misappropriation, trade secret, unfair competition, and other applicable laws. The authors and editors of this work have added value to the underlying factual material herein through one or more of the following: unique and original selection, coordination, expression, arrangement, and classification of the information. All rights to this publication will be vigorously defended.

Copyright © 1999
Gale Research
27500 Drake Rd.
Farmington Hills, MI 48331-3535

All rights reserved including the right of reproduction in whole or in part in any form.

ISBN 0-7876-2725-9
ISSN 1094-7019

Printed in the United States of America.
10 9 8 7 6 5 4 3 2 1

The Highwayman

Alfred Noyes 1907

Introduction

According to his own report, Alfred Noyes wrote "The Highwayman" over a two-day period in 1904 when he was 24 years old. (The poem was published in 1907 in the collection *Forty Singing Seamen and Other Poems.*) "The Highwayman" is a romantic ballad, which means that it is a narrative poem that celebrates passion and adventure. Set in the England of King George III, the poem tells the story of a highwayman, or robber, who has fallen in love with Bess, an innkeeper's beautiful daughter. The lovers are betrayed by a jealous stablehand, and soldiers attempt to trap the highwayman by taking Bess hostage. In an oddly sadistic scene, the soldiers tie Bess up with a gun pointing into her chest, and then wait in ambush for the highwayman. When Bess hears the highwayman approaching, she warns him by shooting herself; he hears the gunshot and escapes. The soldiers pursue him, however, and he, too, is killed. The poem is notable for the way in which it reverses our expectations concerning light and dark imagery. Ordinarily, we think of the clarity of daylight in positive terms. In "The Highwayman," however, Noyes associates the daylight with the destructive powers of mankind, and he identifies the nighttime with the mysterious forces of nature.

Although Noyes wrote "The Highwayman" at the beginning of the Modernist period, the poem seems more characteristic of the Victorian period. The poem is notable for its logical narrative structure and its vivid, highly detailed descriptions —elements the Modernists tended to avoid. Noyes, however, considered himself a traditionalist and rejected the poetic innovations of the Modernists. Deeply religious, Noyes also disapproved of the explicit violence and sexuality that was sometimes evident in his contemporaries' work. "The Highwayman," then, represents something of an anomaly in Noyes's career, for it derives much of its narrative tension and excitement not only from its bloody conclusion, but from its sexually charged atmosphere.

Author Biography

Noyes was born in Wolverhampton, England, on September 16, 1880. His father Alfred was a grocer who later became a teacher. His mother Amelia Adams Rawley Noyes developed a nervous disorder that left her an invalid following the birth of the last of her three sons. Despite this, Noyes always maintained that his childhood was a happy one. He attended school in Wales and later attended Oxford University, leaving without earning a degree. Noyes was considered the most popular poet of his time, with much of the appeal of his early poetry stemming from his optimistic and patriotic worldview. His first collection of poetry, *The Loom of Years,* was published in 1902. In 1904 Noyes wrote "The Highwayman," one of his most popular poems, in two days. In 1907, he married Garnett Daniels, an American, and together they sometimes resided in the United States.

During World War I, Noyes turned his interest to writing fiction, particularly fiction with paranormal and psychic themes. He was named a Commander of the Order of the British Empire in 1918, in part for his work as a reporter for the International News Service during the war. Noyes served as Murray Professor of Literature at Princeton University from 1914 until 1923 (except for his stint as a reporter during the war). Among his students were F. Scott Fitzgerald, Edmund Wilson, and John Peale Bishop. His wife died in

1926, and the following year he married Mary Angela Mayne WeldBlundell. In addition to Mary's daughter by her first marriage, Agnes, the couple had three children together—Henry, Veronica, and Margaret. Noyes's already considerable interest in religion grew, and during the 1930s he came to believe, like the Romantic poets, that nature is a parable directing the individual toward spiritual truth. In 1942 Noyes lost his eyesight to glaucoma, which limited his literary activity to compiling and revising his poems for inclusion in volumes of collected works. Noyes died on June 23, 1958.

Poem Summary

Lines 1-6

The first stanza establishes the stormy tone that will pervade the entire poem. On its most basic level, the stanza describes a windy night and the highwayman's approach on horseback. But in describing the violent wind, Noyes uses images that we might just as easily associate with stormy waters: "a torrent of darkness" and "cloudy seas." By attributing sea-like characteristics to the wind, Noyes magnifies its intensity. He also creates a world that seems oddly unsettled: not only is the ocean confused with the wind, but even the moon itself seems unstable—it is "tossed" about in the sky. It is from this wildly disordered nighttime world that the highwayman first emerges. That is, from the start, we associate the highwayman with the chaotic and mysterious forces of nature.

Lines 7-12

Noyes devotes an entire stanza to describing the highwayman's clothing. We can gather from these lines that the highwayman is a sexy, fashionable dresser. Although Noyes draws our attention to the highwayman's weapons, they appear more decorative than functional: his pistols and sword (which are really the tools of his trade!) "twinkle." Note that the word "twinkle" (which rhymes with "wrinkle" in the middle of the third line) is repeated three times. With his sparkling weapons, the highwayman himself seems almost like one of the stars in the "jewelled sky."

Lines 13-18

In the third stanza, the highwayman arrives at the inn. The repetition of the hard "c" and "k" sounds in the first line mimics the sound of the horse's hooves on the cobblestones; this repetition of stressed consonants is called alliteration. The third stanza also offers an excellent example of narrative compression: that is, Noyes manages to convey a lot of information in a very few lines. Not only does Noyes inform us that Bess opens the window to the highwayman, but through careful diction he suggests that Bess and the highwayman are already lovers. Bess is "waiting" for the highwayman, which implies that she had expected his arrival, and she is braiding a "love-knot," or token of love, into her hair. Noyes makes careful use of color in these lines: with her sensual black eyes and long black hair, Bess—like the highwayman—is also identified with the night. Moreover, both the highwayman and Bess wear a dark red article of clothing (the highwayman's jacket is "claret" velvet): this color effectively foreshadows the bloody end to which they will each come.

Lines 19-24

The fourth stanza introduces Tim, a jealous stablehand who is spying on Bess and the highwayman. Noyes repeats the word "dark" twice in the first line; we are no longer aware of the moonlight that illumined the first three stanzas. Oddly, the only mention of light in this stanza is Tim's sickly white face. Noyes has reversed our normal expectations: usually, we associate the dark with evil and the light with good; here, however, the light seems dangerous and forbidding.

Lines 25-30

Still underneath her window, the highwayman tells Bess about the robbery he plans to commit later that night (a conversation that Tim the ostler overhears). Noyes continues to establish the highwayman as a creature of the night: not only does the highwayman intend to return to Bess before daybreak, but his greatest concern is being pursued "through the day." Notice the recurrence of the phrase "by moonlight" in the last three lines of the stanza. The first two instances occur in the two trimeter lines; the third occurs in the first half of the final hexameter line. By echoing the same three-stressed phrase three times, Noyes creates a climactic effect. This climactic build prepares us for the dramatic stanza which follows.

Lines 31-36

This stanza concludes the first part of the poem. In it, the highwayman bids farewell to Bess and rides off to the west of England—probably toward Wales (where Noyes himself grew up). The description of their farewell is at once highly sensual and sexually charged. As Bess's long hair spills over the highwayman's face, we are told that it "burnt like a brand." A brand is a tool used to burn an identifying mark in the flesh, and we have a sense here that, in parting, the two lovers have become permanently identified with each other. Notice, too, the recurrence of the water imagery that appeared in the first stanza. Bess's hair is described as a "cascade," or waterfall, and as having "waves." By reinvoking this water imagery, Noyes links Bess to the stormy, windy night. At the end of Part One, then, Noyes has not only portrayed the passionate bond between the highwayman and Bess, but he has also associated both the lovers with the chaotic and dark night.

Media Adaptations

- Three poems by Noyes, "Sherwood," his poem about Robin Hood; "The Barrel-Organ," which was perhaps his best-known poem in his lifetime; and "Epilogue," from *The Flower of Old Japan;* were included in Louis Untermeyer's 1920 anthology *Modern British Poetry.* The collection is available on-line at http://www.columbia.edu/acis/bartleby/n

- Phil Ochs set "The Highwayman" to music and recorded it on his 1965 album, *I Ain't Marching Anymore.* The album has been re-released by Hannibal.

Lines 37-42

The narrative resumes at sunset the following day; almost a full day has passed, but the highwayman has not yet returned. Instead, a whole troop of British soldiers appear, warned, no doubt, by Tim. Note the many ways in which this stanza echoes the very first stanza of the poem: the second lines of both stanzas mention the moon; the third lines describe the "road" as a "ribbon" on the "purple moor"; in the fourth, fifth, and sixth lines, a present participle verb, separated by dashes, is repeated four times ("riding" in the first stanza and "marching" here); and both stanzas conclude with the "old inn-door" being approached. The first stanza heralded the appearance of the highwayman. Given the way this stanza so closely echoes the first, we expect him to reappear. It is all the more disquieting, then, when in his place the red-coats appear.

Lines 43-48

This stanza is extraordinarily violent. It begins with a violation of the landlord himself: the soldiers barge into the inn and take his ale. More important, the red-coats gag and tie up Bess—an action that is deliberately suggestive of sexual violence. Note the difference between the highwayman's and the soldiers' treatment of Bess. We would expect the soldiers (the representatives of the King) to be orderly and law-abiding and the highwayman (a criminal) to be cruel and uncaring. Exactly the opposite is true. Again we see Noyes reversing our expectations.

Lines 49-54

The images of sexual violence and abuse become even more pronounced as the soldiers mock and then kiss Bess. They "tie her up to attention" with a gun pointed to her chest—a grotesque parody of a soldier. This stanza is remarkable for its sadistic overtones: given Noyes's otherwise conservative attitudes toward the portrayal of sexuality and violence, one wonders why he would have written such a cruel scene. At best, we can say that the soldiers' behavior serves as a useful contrast to the highwayman's. Their repulsiveness makes us appreciate even more the purity of the highwayman's love for Bess. (Note that in the third line the highwayman is described as "dead," even though he has not yet been killed. For a moment, we see the situation through Bess's eyes: to her, the highwayman's death is so inevitable that she already thinks of him as dead.)

Lines 56-61

Having recognized that the highwayman will certainly be killed if he reaches the inn, Bess attempts to warn him. She strains against the rope until she is able to reach the trigger. In describing this scene, Noyes uses a series of discordant, grating rhymes: "good" and "blood"; "midnight" and "it"; "years" and "hers." "Good" and "blood" are called eye rhymes; the others are called off rhymes. All create a sense that something is, in fact, slightly "off" or wrong—no accident, considering the terribly wrong act of suicide that Bess is about to commit.

Lines 62-67

The first line of this stanza echoes the last line of the previous stanza, reminding us that Bess only needs to be able to reach the trigger in order to kill herself. In the second line, we are told that Bess "stood up to attention," an odd echo of line 49, which described the soldiers' mocking treatment of her. In this context, however, the sense of the phrase is transformed: rather than being demeaned, Bess grows in nobility as she prepares to sacrifice herself for her lover. The reference to "blood" in the last line of the stanza warns us that Bess's own blood will soon be spilled. This line also reminds us of the permanent bond between the two lovers: we are told the pulse of the blood in Bess's veins "throbs" to the same beat as her lover's "refrain." It is not until the following stanza, however, that we are told what the highwayman's "refrain" is.

Lines 68-73

We are now told that the "refrain" is actually the sound of the highwayman's horses' hoofs (and in fact, the rhythm of a fast heartbeat can feel like the beat of horses' hoofs). For the second time in the poem, we hear the highwayman approaching the inn. Noyes again uses the same formula that he used in the first stanza to describe the highwayman's approach: the third line repeats the image of a "ribbon of moonlight"; and the fourth and fifth lines repeat the word "riding" three times. But here Noyes makes a notable change. In the first stanza, the word "riding" also appears in the final line: it signals the highwayman's arrival at the inn door. In this stanza, Noyes substitutes the word "priming" for "riding." This unexpected substitution drives home the idea that instead of arriving at the inn-door, the highwayman will meet the "primed" muskets of the soldiers.

Lines 74-79

Just as the highwayman is about to be shot, Bess pulls the trigger and kills herself. Note, however, that the gun "shatters" not only Bess's chest, but the "moonlight" itself. Because both Bess and the highwayman are so closely identified with the moonlight, Bess's death seems to disrupt the entire night world. Note, moreover, the caesura, or break, in the last line of the stanza. Just as the moonlight has become shattered, or broken, the rhythm of the line itself has been shattered.

Lines 80-85

The highwayman hears the gunshot and escapes, not realizing that Bess has killed herself. Notably, he does not learn the truth until the next morning—and daylight. Bess, he is told, "died in the darkness." Her death signals an end to the mysterious and sensual nighttime world she and her lover had inhabited. Bess's death thrusts the poem into the glaring light of day; Noyes's diction underscores the unpleasant nature of the "whiteness" associated with the daylight hours. When the highwayman learns of Bess's death, for instance, he "blanches," or turns white, with dread.

Lines 86-91

The imagery of this stanza reminds us that we are now indeed in the ugly daylight world dominated by the soldiers: no longer a "ribbon of moonlight," the road is "white" and "smoking." If the highwayman had governed the nighttime world, he is clearly out of his element in the daylight. With no trouble, the soldiers pursue and shoot him: he dies in the very "highway" he had once ruled. He has been reduced from the mysterious "highway *man*" to a *"dog* on the highway."

Lines 92-103

The final two stanzas repeat, almost word for word, the first and third stanzas of the poem. After the bloody carnage of Part Two, these lines take on added dimension. On one level, they bring us full circle to the beginning of the poem, reminding us of the pure love that Bess and the highwayman once shared. On another level, the repetition of these lines suggests that despite the carnage, the bond between the two lovers is so strong that even death cannot destroy it. In spirit—and in our imaginations—the renegade highwayman will forever be riding up the inn-door, where Bess will forever be there to welcome him. One is left to wonder then, where the victory lies: With the cruel and ugly powers of the day? Or with the mysterious forces of the night?

Themes

Love and Passion

Above all else, "The Highwayman" is a poem that celebrates the passionate love of its two central characters. The poem's subject is revealed in the third stanza, when the highwayman first arrives at Bess's window. Although it is the middle of the night and the inn is "locked and barred," Bess has eagerly anticipated his arrival by tying a "dark red love-knot" in her hair. (The color red, which is associated with intense passion, recurs throughout the poem: in Bess's red lips, the highwayman's red coat, and the color of their blood.) The scene at Bess's window is charged with images of sensual love—the moonlight, Bess's perfumed hair, and the highwayman's face which "burn[s] like a brand." The fact that the two lovers can barely touch—"he scarce could reach her hand"—simply intensifies the feeling of passion. The highwayman can only kiss the "sweet black cascade of perfume" that is Bess's hair. Their brief but romantic encounter builds up anticipation for their next meeting. Before leaving her, the highwayman makes a fateful promise that reveals the depth of his love and foreshadows his final sacrifice: "I'll come to thee by moonlight," he tells her, "though hell should bar the way."

The first part of "The Highwayman"

introduces the notion of romantic love, but the high drama of the second part manifests it. Held prisoner by soldiers, Bess is used to lay a trap for the highwayman and is forced to watch as they prepare to murder him. She strains against her bonds, oblivious to the pain, "till her fingers were wet with sweat or blood." As the highwayman approaches, her finger pulls the trigger of the rifle bound against her. Its report warns the highwayman but kills Bess.

Bess's action expresses the epitome of the nineteenth-century Romantics' concept of a love so intense and unselfish that one is willing to die for another. The Romantics believed that love had a religious, almost mystical quality. In this context, passion took the place of grace, and the loved one took the place of God. In the Middle Ages, it was believed a saint transfigured by God's grace would take on a holy glow. Just before she kills herself, Bess is transfigured by love: "Her face was like a light." After her death, Bess is "drenched with her own red blood," which symbolizes Bess's passion for the highwayman.

The highwayman loves Bess just as passionately. After hearing of her death, he makes good on his promise to return. The highwayman too is overwhelmed by his love, and like Bess's final moments, his have religious overtones. But the highwayman is no calm saint; rather he seems possessed by the devil—"spurred like a madman, shrieking a curse." Riding back to Bess, expressing his anguish with violence, he brandishes his weapon for the first time. He disregards his own safety as he rushes back; his reckless and violent ride seems as much a suicide as when Bess pulled the musket trigger. He dies on the highway "like a dog": his love, like Bess's, is sealed in his own blood.

The Romantics, however, believed that a passionate, true love conquered all. Because their love is so strong and genuine, death is not able to separate Bess and her highwayman. On the contrary, it unites them forever. The power of their love has made them immortal, and on dark and stormy nights their love is renewed at the inn. As the poem ends, Bess is eternally plaiting a love-knot in her hair for the highwayman.

The Outlaw

The outlaw held an important place in the Romantic imagination. The Romantics maintained that the rules and norms of bourgeois society—such as money lust and the denial of feelings—made it impossible to experience life to the fullest. Far from being a criminal, the outlaw had the courage to flaunt society's rules. As a result, he won deeper insight into the world and himself, and he had more genuine emotional experience than ordinary people. In general, the outlaw lived a more worthwhile life.

Topics for Further Study

- Write a scene in which the highwayman is robbing some victims at gunpoint. Is he as charming as when we see him in this poem, or is he ruthless when he works? Does he rob for personal gain or political principle? Are the people he robs terrified or charmed?

- What do you think Tim the ostler, mentioned in stanza 3, has to do with this situation? Why does Noyes mention him? What do you think happened to him when the poem was over.

Both the highwayman and Bess are outlaws in this tradition. The highwayman is literally an outlaw who prowls the roads robbing travelers. But the poem hints that his actions are more adventure than crime. The gold he will bring Bess is not booty, it is his "prize," or his reward for meeting a challenge successfully. In the first stanza of the poem he is associated with the moon, which is depicted as a "galleon," or the vessel in which pirates travel. He dresses like an outsider as well, wearing, for instance, "a French cocked-hat" rather than an English one.

Bess and the highwayman are outsiders in other ways as well. They meet in the dead of night when, according to tradition, normal daytime rules are suspended. Their love is a secret one, hidden from daytime view. At least, they think it is; but in fact, Tim the ostler knows about them. Tim views the highwayman and Bess with the prejudice, suspicion, and disapproval of the middle-class world. With jealousy, as well, for he lusts after Bess, but is too cowardly to approach her. The unhealthiness of Tim's feelings is reflected in his physical appearance, which is in stark contrast to the gallant and debonair impression the highwayman makes. Tim is pale, sickly, degenerate, and "his eyes were hollows of madness." What's more, he is "dumb as a dog." He cannot comprehend the life or emotions of Bess and the highwayman although he is directly confronted with them.

The highwayman is associated with the night, but also with goodness and purity of feeling. His weapons are not threatening, they merely "twinkle" at his sides. He does not use them—at least not until after Bess's death. The highwayman's essential goodness is thrown into sharp relief by the sadistic soldiers who barge into the inn, drink without paying, and take Bess hostage. The highwayman is content merely to breath the perfume from Bess's hair because he loves her. In contrast, the soldiers mistreat her; they bind her to her bed with a musket tied beneath her bosom. After they bind and gag her, they commit a symbolic rape by forcing their kisses upon her. Most horribly, she is forced to watch as they prepare to murder her lover. The soldiers are supposed to enforce and uphold the law. Their immoral behavior shows just how meaningless their daytime laws really are. Noyes implies that it is no crime to oppose these men, but rather, it is honorable to live outside the law in such a world.

Style

"The Highwayman" is composed of six-line stanzas that rhyme in an *aabccb* pattern. Notice, however, that the "c" rhymes actually repeat the same word: "twinkle" and "twinkle," for instance, in the second stanza. In fact, one of the most noteworthy features of this poem is its use of repetition. Throughout the poem, Noyes reinvokes key words, phrases, and images: the word "moonlight," for example, appears nineteen times in the poem. Noyes also echoes individual sounds by using alliteration and assonance in literally every stanza. These different forms of repetition intensify the poem's dramatic impact.

The poem is written in hexameters, which means that each line has six stressed syllables. If we scan, or identify the stresses in the first line of the poem, for instance, it appears as follows:

> The **wind** was a **tor**ent of **dark**ness **among** the **gusty trees.**

Try reading the line aloud. Its fast and heavily pulsing rhythm contributes to the poem's energy.

Note, however, that the fourth and fifth lines (the "c" rhymed lines) generally each have only three stresses, a form of meter called trimeter. Look, for instance, at the two trimeter lines from the second stanza:

And he **rode** with a **jew**elled **twin**kle
His **pis**tol **butts** a-**twin**kle.

For purposes of scansion, we might simply regard these two trimeter, or three-stressed lines, as one hexameter, or six-stressed line. Doing so, however, would ignore the dramatic effect of the trimeters. Because the two trimeter lines are, in fact, so short—and because they repeat each other—they must be read very quickly. In fact, if you read them aloud, you will notice that it is easy to become breathless. This sense of breathlessness adds to the excitement and passion of the poem.

Historical Context

In 1907, when "The Highwayman" was first published, a period of profound transition was taking place throughout English society; this included the areas of politics, international relations, economics, literature, and ultimately in the self-image of the English. The most notable event during this period of transition was the death of Queen Victoria, who had reigned over Britain for more than 62 years, in January of 1901. Her death symbolized the end of the pastoral Britain that existed before the onset of the Industrial Revolution and heralded a new century rife with uncertainty.

Queen Victoria had been stabilizing force in European politics as well; she was the matriarch of many European royal families through the marriages of her children and grandchildren. In that role, she linked isolationist-minded Britain with the continent. In particular, she had kept relations with Britain's main European rival, Germany, from becoming too tense.

During the last quarter of the nineteenth century, Germany's development of strong steel, coal, machine-building, and railroad industries challenged Britain's century-long predominance in industry. Even more critically, Germany had begun an accelerated ship-building program designed to create a German Navy equal to England's. These developments made the English uneasy. They sensed both an economic threat to their dominant position in the world and a military threat to their security. Although the Germans claimed their navy would pose no threat to the British, this failed to settle their uneasiness, because a strong navy could be used to pursue German colonial interests abroad.

Although the British Empire encompassed some 11 million square miles of territory on every continent, it was showing early signs of disintegration in the first decade of the century. Britain had fought an unpopular and controversial colonial war against Boer settlers in South Africa between 1899 and 1902. Even though Britain won the war, the Transvaal and Orange Free State (now regions of South Africa) were each granted self-government shortly after the victory. This foreshadowed Britain's losses of other parts of the Empire later in the twentieth century.

In 1902 England signed the Anglo-Japanese Alliance with Japan. It was significant in that it was the first time a European nation had recognized a non-European nation as diplomatically equal. Historians consider it one of the most important diplomatic agreements of modern times. It thrust Japan out of its long isolation and onto the world stage. The Alliance provided that Japan would attempt to suppress Russian invasions of China and Korea. Two years later the Russo-Japanese War broke out; in 1905 Japan emerged victorious. That a European nation, even one in Russia's decrepit condition, could be defeated by an Asian country was completely unexpected. By the end of the

1920s, Japan had strengthened its military and laid plans for an empire of its own in the Pacific. Interestingly, a year after the treaty was signed, Noyes published his collection *The Flower of Old Japan.*

In 1900 English poetry was felt to be on the ebb. During the 1800s poetry had enjoyed a level of popularity in England unmatched before or since. But the poets who were responsible for much of that popularity were gone: Alfred Lord Tennyson and Robert Browning were dead, and other poets, including A. C. Swinburne and George Meredith, were past their primes. No new writers of their genre had risen to take their place and a successor was eagerly awaited. When Alfred Noyes published his first books of poetry between 1902 and 1905, he was eagerly hailed at the next great English poet who would take the tradition over into the twentieth century. His work was firmly rooted in nineteenth-century poetic aesthetics however, and by the middle of the next decade, he was overtaken by modernist poets such as T. S. Eliot and Ezra Pound.

Compare & Contrast

- **1907:** Great Britain permits self-rule in the Orange Free State in South Africa leading to the institutionalization of Apartheid.

  Today: Apartheid has ended, but whites and blacks in South Africa continue to deal with its legacy as the controversial Truth and Reconciliation Committee investigates atrocities committed by the former government.

- **1907:** The United States enters a brief economic depression and the Panic of 1907 hits. Under the leadership of financier J. P. Morgan, the quick infusion of millions of dollars into the economy saves it from more serious problems.

  Today: A serious recession in Pacific Rim nations, including Japan, Korea, Indonesia, and Singapore, destabilizes local governments and threatens to spread to the rest of the world.

- **1907:** Busses and taxicabs are introduced in New York City.

  Today: Despite warnings about pollution and global warming, most Americans still own and drive a private automobile.

- **1907:** President Theodore Roosevelt creates approximately 16 million acres of federal forest land. The forests are supposed to remain untouched by lumber interests.

  Today: More than 377,000 miles of logging roads—eight times the length of the national highway system—have been cut into national forests so the timber industry can harvest trees.

- **1907:** Nearly 1.29 million immigrants are admitted to the United States, an all-time high.

  Today: About 915,900 immigrants entered the country in 1996, despite pressure from various groups to place tighter governmental restrictions on entry requirements.

Critical Overview

In 1906, *The Bookman* described Noyes's poetry as having "music, colour, and sparkle." In many ways, this response characterizes later critical reactions to "The Highwayman." Through the years, critics have appreciated the poem's compelling narrative and its metrical energy. In his book on Alfred Noyes, Walter Jerrold praises the poem for its "popular appeal" and its "dramatic intensity." Jerrold goes on to call the poem "a fine rendering of something finely done." Patrick Braybrooke, in *Some Victorian and Georgian Catholics: Their Art and Outlook,* also praises the poem for its popular appeal. He notes that the verse itself recreates the feel of someone riding. He characterizes the poem, moreover, "as an absolute model of careful and skilled romanticism." Braybrooke does qualify his praise, however, commenting that it would be inaccurate "to observe that Noyes is a poet who can transcend beauty and produce poetry of a 'terrific nature.'" Instead, Braybrooke commends Noyes for "know[ing] the limits of his craft" and for having "a tremendous sense ... of the romantic."

What Do I Read Next?

- Noyes wrote poetry rooted in the traditions of the past and was extremely hostile to the modernist poets. His harsh criticism of their work can be found in his book *Some Aspects of Modern Poetry.*

- Noyes was often compared as a poet to Rudyard Kipling, who celebrated the British Empire in his poems and stories. *The Phantom 'Rickshaw, and Other Tales* contains stories of the fantastic and supernatural, often set in exotic lands.

- Just before Noyes celebrated the outlaw in "The Highwayman," Thorstein Veblen published *A Theory of the Leisure Class,* a sarcastic, highly readable critique of middle-class consumer society.

- Noyes was seen as the heir to Poet Laureate Alfred Lord Tennyson. Tennyson's *Idylls of the King,* a verse treatment of the story of King Arthur, offers a different viewpoint on love than Noyes's. The forbidden love of Lancelot and Queen Guinevere leads to the fall of Camelot.

- *A Modern Utopia* by H.G. Wells was published two years before Noyes's poem. Rather than turning back to the romantic past in the face of rapid change, Wells looked forward to the improvements science, technology, and socialism would bring in the future.

Sources

"The Bookman Gallery: Alfred Noyes," in *The Bookman,* Vol. 30, No. 180, September 1906, pp. 199-200.

Braybrooke, Patrick, "Alfred Noyes: Poet and Romantic," in his *Some Victorian and Georgian Catholics: Their Art and Outlook,* Burns Oates & Washbourne Ltd., 1932, pp. 171-202, reprinted by Books for Libraries Press, Inc., 1966; distributed by Arno Press, Inc.

Davison, Edward Lewis, *Some Modern Poets and other Critical Essays,* Freeport, NY: Books for Libraries, 1968.

Kernahan, Coulson, *Six Famous Living Poets,* Freeport, NY: Books for Libraries, 1968.

For Further Study

Brenner, Rica, *Ten Modern Poets,* Freeport, NY: Books for Libraries, 1968.

> A readable overview of Noyes's poetic output up to 1930.

Jerrold, Walter, in his *Alfred Noyes,* Harold Shaylor, 1930, 251 p.

> A highly appreciative consideration of Noyes's work—in particular his longer, historical poems—that calles the poet the heir to Tennyson and Browning.

Saul, G. B., "Yeats, Noyes and Day Lewis," in *Notes and Queries,* No. 195, 1950.

> A comparison of three poets who dealt explicitly with religious material in their works.

Lightning Source UK Ltd.
Milton Keynes UK
UKHW021339250319
339840UK00009B/212/P